Paul Revere

SON OF LIBERTY

2.50

Paul Revere

SON OF LIBERTY

by Keith Brandt
illustrated by Francis Livingston

Troll Associates

Library of Congress Cataloging in Publication Data

Brandt, Keith (date)
    Paul Revere, son of liberty.

    Summary: Recounts the early life of the boy who grew
up to become a famous silversmith and Revolutionary War
patriot.
    1. Revere, Paul, 1735-1818—Juvenile literature.
2. Massachusetts—History—Revolution, 1775-1783—
Juvenile literature.   3. Statesmen—Massachusetts—
Biography—Juvenile literature.   4. Massachusetts—
Biography—Juvenile literature.   [1. Revere, Paul, 1735-
1818.   2. United States—History—Revolution, 1775-1783
—Biography.   3. Silversmiths]   I. Livingston, Francis,
ill.   II. Title.
F69.R43B7   973.3 '311 '0924 [B] [92]   81-23147
ISBN 0-89375-766-7   AACR2
ISBN 0-89375-767-5 (pbk.)

10   9   8   7   6   5   4   3   2

Paul Revere

SON OF LIBERTY

The Rivoire family of Riauchaud, France, lived well. Their home was a sturdy stone house, surrounded by vineyards that produced fine grapes. They were healthy, honest, well-liked people. Even so, the Rivoires were not happy. They always lived in fear that their secret would be discovered. For the Rivoires were Huguenots —a group belonging to the Protestant faith.

In France at that time, Protestants were thrown into prison or driven from the country. Their churches were closed, and they could not hold religious services. They were strangers in their own land.

The Rivoires, like many other French Protestants, did not give in. They practiced their faith and baptized their children in secret. They hoped and prayed for religious freedom. But conditions only grew worse.

Then, in 1715, the Rivoires made an important decision. They were too old to leave their homeland and start over somewhere else. But it was decided their thirteen-year-old son, Apollos, should go where he could live in freedom. He was put on a small ship that took him to the English island of Guernsey. There, his Uncle Simon arranged for his passage to America.

"In a few weeks you will be in the city called Boston, and your new life will begin," Simon told his young nephew. "It will be a good life if you do whatever Mr. Coney tells you. So long as you are his apprentice, he is your master in everything. For seven years you will work in his shop and learn to be a fine silversmith. Then, one day, the name *Rivoire* will be honored."

"Seven years before I will be really free," sighed Apollos. He looked at the ship he was about to board.

"It is true that you will have to obey Mr. Coney," his uncle said. "But you will be free in the ways that really matter. In the city where you will live, you will be free to go to your church. And you will be free to marry in your own faith, and raise your children to be free citizens in that new world."

The great sailing ship carrying Apollos Rivoire reached Boston Harbor and anchored at Long Wharf. Standing at the ship's rail, the boy gaped at the 2,000-foot-long pier. There were places for many ships to dock, shops of all kinds, warehouses, auction halls, rope-makers, and carpenters. There were merchants wearing powdered wigs and clothing trimmed with fine lace...sailors hurrying off to spend time in merry Boston...porters staggering down gangplanks, their backs bent under the weight of heavy trunks. Why, Long Wharf, all by itself, was bigger than Apollos's whole village!

11

The years that followed brought many changes in the life of Apollos Rivoire. He served out his apprenticeship with Mr. Coney, then became a master silversmith with his own shop. He married Deborah Hitchbourn. And he even changed his name to make it easier for his customers to say. Apollos Rivoire became Paul Revere. This was also the name he gave to his first son, born on January 1, 1735.

When he was a child, young Paul Revere loved to hear his father's stories about the past. The boy would sit in the small silversmith's shop on Fish Street, watching his father make a serving tray from the shiny metal. Mr. Revere talked as he worked. Paul leaned close to hear every word.

"My family's home in France is made of thick, strong stone," said Mr. Revere. "It has stood for many centuries. A fire would not destroy it."

"It must be far better than the wooden houses we have here in Boston," Paul said, wishing they lived in a stone house. "There are so many fires here."

His father nodded. "Yes, but there are things more important than what a house is made of. All the castles, the stone bridges, the handsome paved streets of France—none of them is worth anything if you are not free."

"Is that what Uncle Thomas means when he says we don't need a king?" asked the boy.

Mr. Revere smiled. "Your uncle wants to overthrow our British king right now," he said.

15

"I think it will happen, but not yet. Perhaps when you are a man." He rumpled Paul's hair. "Now, run along, see if your mother needs you."

The dark-eyed boy jumped down from the wooden stool and ran next door, into the Revere kitchen. He sniffed the air and shouted happily, "Oh, Mama! Roast duck and suet pudding. I'm so hungry!"

Paul's mother laughed and said, "Dinner will be ready soon—if I can finish my cooking. Now you must help by minding the little ones."

Paul had just the thing to keep his younger brothers and sisters busy. Digging into a pocket, he pulled out a leather pouch filled with marbles. "Come on," he called to them. "I have a new game to show you."

His eyes sparkling, Paul led the children to a corner of the room away from his mother. There, he smoothed a place in the sandy dirt floor and spilled out the marbles. Soon everyone was playing the game Paul had learned from one of his schoolmates that morning.

16

The shrieks and giggles of the children rang through the house. "Paul is only nine, yet he acts as grown-up as a man," Deborah said to her mother as she helped prepare the duck for roasting. Deborah was eleven, the oldest of the Revere children.

"That's true," Mrs. Revere agreed. "And that is why your father says he will be a successful tradesman someday."

It was a warm spring afternoon, and the kitchen door was wide open. In the small back yard, chickens pecked at the corn kernels Paul had spread for them. A pig, lying in the shade of an elm tree, grunted in its sleep. The Reveres' dog was also lying down, until it heard the children laughing and bounded into the house.

The dog was very small. It had to be. There was a law, in Boston, that forbade the keeping of dogs that stood higher than ten inches. It was all right for people living in the countryside to have big dogs. But in the city of Boston, they were not allowed.

It was a sensible law. In those days, butchers hung their meats out in the street, where shoppers could see what was being sold. Before the dog law was passed, big dogs ran loose. And they often stole pieces of meat. The angry butchers spoke to the town council about the problem. This resulted, in 1728, in the passage of the ten-inch-dog law.

Even though 15,000 people lived in Boston, it was like a small town in many ways. Pigs, chickens, dogs, and cats roamed the streets. The children also ran free. They might wander down to the docks to watch the ships being loaded and unloaded. Or go for a swim in Mill Cove. Or watch the British soldiers, in their bright red coats, marching around the Commons. The Commons was an open field, where cows and sheep grazed.

One of the children's favorite games was making believe they were pirates or sailors at sea. It would have been just tame fun if they had played it on land. But that wasn't the way the game was played. Instead, the boys would go to the docks and climb aboard the sailing ships when nobody was around.

Once aboard, they would duel with sticks and pretend to fire cannons. But the real thrill was to climb the ship's rigging. These were rope ladders that stretched from the deck to the high masts and sails. There were also ropes to swing on. And even more dangerous than climbing the rope ladders, the children would shinny across the heavy wooden poles that held the sails.

Paul knew that playing on the ships was risky. One of his own cousins had fallen from the rigging and been killed. Paul's parents warned him to stay away from the ships, but he didn't listen. Then one day Paul and another boy were caught by a ship's captain. He ordered them down to the deck.

"This is the last time you'll hear a warning from me," the captain growled. "And it's the last time you'll try that climbing. Because the next time you do, I'll give you the hiding of your lives. Then I'll take you home and watch your fathers do the same—or worse!"

That was the last time Paul Revere ever climbed a ship's rigging!

But it wasn't often that Paul got into trouble. He was very grown-up for his age, and very serious about his responsibilities.

At North Writing School, Paul worked as hard as any of the students. He had started at the two-room schoolhouse when he was eight years old. Paul liked school. One of the reasons was that Zachariah Hicks, the schoolmaster, was a good teacher. Paul thought he was strict but fair. When the boys misbehaved, he would punish them with a birch rod. But he was also quick to reward them with praise and tasty seed cakes when they learned well and behaved like "proper gentlemen."

North Writing School was a "free public school," but parents had to pay five shillings for each child who attended. This money was for "firing." That meant buying firewood for the stove that heated the schoolhouse in the long and cold New England winters.

In Mr. Hicks's class, Paul learned reading, grammar, spelling, and some arithmetic. There were no summer vacations—school was held year-round. The only official holidays were Sundays and election days.

Even though there wasn't much time off from school, Paul knew that he, like most of his friends, would get no more than five years of education. In those days, nearly every boy went to work as an apprentice at the age of thirteen. Only the children of rich families went on to further schooling, where they would prepare for college. Only in rare cases did one of the poorer boys get to study at a higher level.

But not all of Paul's education took place in the classroom. He kept his ears open to hear the sailors talk about the exciting, faraway places they had visited. He heard Mr. Revere and his friends argue angrily about the British government's latest taxes upon the colonies. Sometimes, on Sundays, he went to West Street Church and listened to Reverend Jonathan Mayhew's sermons. In a strong voice, Mayhew reminded his audience that it was the *duty* of oppressed people everywhere to rebel against an unjust king.

Mayhew's sermons sent shock waves through Boston. Many people might agree with him, but to speak those ideas out loud was treason! Yet he spoke them, and no thunderbolt from England struck him dead. And soon, others began speaking *their* minds. It was for this reason that, years later, John Adams called Mayhew's sermons "the opening gun of the Revolution."

The Boston in which Paul lived was filled with bitterness against England. The British government passed one harsh law after another against the colonies. For example, the fishermen of Massachusetts colony were not allowed to ship and sell their fish to any other colony (or anywhere else in the world). If Virginia or another colony wanted to import fish, the fish had to be sent all the way across the Atlantic Ocean from England. In this way, English fishermen—and certain government officials—made a very nice profit.

Bostonians also paid heavy taxes to England on everything they imported, everything they exported, and everything they made, bought, or sold.

"England is draining us dry," grumbled Paul's uncle, Thomas Hitchbourn. "And, as we all know, when things get tinder-dry, they catch fire. Mind what I say, boy. The fire is coming!"

Once in a while, Paul talked about these
things with his school friends. But mostly he
listened to the older people, did his chores,
learned his lessons, and spent his free time
playing.

When he turned thirteen, Paul's school days were over. Now he was an apprentice to his father, as his father had been to Mr. Coney. Early every morning, the two of them went to work in the little silversmith shop on Fish Street. Father and son dressed alike, in a simple homespun shirt, leather breeches, and a leather apron. Leather breeches and aprons were worn by many craftsmen. This clothing lasted a long time, and it shielded the wearers from injury as they worked.

The young apprentice began with simple jobs. Paul would sweep the shop several times a day. Each time, he would sift out any silver dust that fell to the floor. Silver was so valuable that Mr. Revere could not afford to let even the tiniest bit be swept into the street.

Paul's other job was to keep the brick furnace stoked with charcoal. The furnace fire was used all day long. Pieces of silver were put in a pot and melted in the furnace. The silversmith would mold the soft, melted metal into something useful—a cup, a bowl, knives and spoons, a tray, buttons, buckles—whatever the customer ordered.

As the silver cooled, it grew hard. Then, if the piece wasn't finished, it would have to be heated and softened again. The silver might have to be softened dozens of times before the object was in its final shape. Then, it might be engraved with a beautiful design. At last, when the object was ready for the customer, it was stamped with the name or trademark of the silversmith.

33

Every bit of work was done by hand, and every object took time to make. There were no machines, as there are today, to stamp out hundreds of buckles or buttons an hour. Paul had to learn to use the silversmith's tools. Most important were the hammers, used for beating the metal into shape, and sharp tools, for cutting designs into the silver.

Paul worked from sunrise to sunset, six days a week. On Sunday all businesses were closed. This was a time for the Reveres to go to the Cockerel Church and spend a pleasant day together at home.

Like the Puritans who had settled the city a century earlier, Bostonians of Paul's time were very serious about religion. Their churches were plain and simple, and so were the services held in them. There weren't many holidays. Even Christmas wasn't celebrated in this colonial city. The Episcopal churches, however, were decorated with evergreen branches at Christmas time. The boughs looked and smelled very nice, and children of all faiths used to go inside the church to see and sniff the greens. Paul and his friends used to visit Christ Church, also called the Old North Church, on Salem Street, every Christmas.

Paul also was fascinated by something else at Christ Church. In the steeple hung eight huge bells. The smallest weighed 620 pounds, the largest was 1,545 pounds. On them was inscribed, "We are the first ring of bells cast for the British Empire in North America." Each of these bells had its own pure and clear sound. Paul loved the sound of those bells.

When he was fifteen, Paul formed a bell-ringing club with six of his friends. Ringing the bells was not easy. A thick rope hung from each of the eight bells. The ringer of a bell had to reach high up on the rope, grab it firmly, and pull down as hard as he could. Then he would let go of the rope. The pulling and letting go of the rope would make the bell swing and ring.

The hardest part of ringing the bells was making them play a song. The bells were numbered 1 through 8. And each song that was played required the bells to be played in a different order. Paul's club had to learn the correct order for many different songs. They also had to time their ringing perfectly, so that one bell would not drown out the sound of another bell. Two hours of practice was hard on the arm and back muscles, but the boys loved every minute of it. They also were glad to get the few shillings the church congregation gave them each week.

Paul and his friends liked being way up in the church steeple. From there they could look out and see all of Boston. And, of course, this meant that the steeple could be seen from everywhere in the city. Little did Paul know then, but this fact would one day be very important in the history of the United States.

In April 1775, when British troops were about to attack the city, Paul would remember the steeple. And he would tell his fellow patriot, Robert Newman, to go up to Old North Church steeple and keep watch. Up there he'd be able to see which way the British were coming. Then, as poet Henry Wadsworth Longfellow wrote, Paul told Newman to

"Hang a lantern aloft in the belfry arch
Of the North Church tower as a
*   signal light—*
One, if by land, and two, if by sea;
And I on the opposite shore will be,
Ready to ride and spread the alarm."

And when the signal came—two lanterns—Paul set out on horseback to spread the word that "The British are coming! Take arms!"

If not for Paul Revere's brave plan that night, the British might have captured some of America's greatest patriots. And if not for his boyhood bell-ringing, Paul might not have known what an excellent "watchtower" the steeple would be.

Spending those hours in the belfry became important to Paul in other ways, too. On summer evenings, before practice began, he enjoyed just looking out over the surrounding city. In one direction, he could see the Charles River, the Common, and Mill Cove. In another direction, he could see all the wharfs and stores along the harbor. Rocking on the harbor's waters were the tall-masted ships of trade, the bulky whalers, and the smaller fishing craft.

From where he stood, Paul could see every street and every house in Boston. He liked to pick out his own house, and those of his friends. The winding, narrow streets and alleys of Boston could even confuse someone who grew up there. But not Paul. He knew the city perfectly—north, east, south, west—from those peaceful hours spent in the steeple.

In later years, Paul would use that knowledge to become an excellent map-maker. His maps of the harbor, of the city streets, and of the countryside around Boston show us just the way those places looked back then.

But all of this was far in the future for the teenager. Most of young Paul's time was spent in the hot, stuffy silversmith shop on Fish Street. Almost every day his father taught him something new. And Paul, a very fast learner, was soon recognized as an unusually skilled silversmith. Mr. Revere had good reason to be proud of his gifted son.

Young Paul's genius was so great that he is regarded as the finest silversmith America has ever known. His designs were—and are—so beautiful that they are as admired in our time as they were more than two hundred years ago.

By the time Paul was in his late teens, he was a better silversmith than Mr. Revere himself. So, when his father died suddenly, in 1754, nineteen-year-old Paul was able to continue the family business.

Paul became a famous silversmith, a brave patriot in the American Revolution, and a leading citizen of his new nation.

Paul was eighty-three when he died in 1818. That morning, and again that evening, the bells in the Old North Church tolled eighty-three times. The clear and pure sounds he loved so deeply rang out to honor one of America's truest sons of liberty.